MADE FOR MORE DEVOTIONAL

MOBILIZING YOUR FAITH FOR EVERYDAY MISSION

A 30-DAY DEVOTIONAL FROM THE BOOK OF EPHESIANS

BY ERIKA RIZKALLAH

Featured Made for More Resources

MADE FOR MORE VISUAL GUIDE

This "read in an hour," visually engaging, resource introduces and integrates three new frameworks to help shift your ministry from a volunteer based *"we can do it you can help"* approach to a *"you can do it, we can help"* missionary focused approach.

MORE

BE-DO-GO Framework

Who and I created to BE?
What I am made to DO?
Where am I to GO?

MADE FOR MORE BIBLE STUDY

The Six Shifts of Mobilization Framework

Bible study for staff & elders that highlights six key shifts that are necessary to create a healthy culture of mobilization.

THE MOBILIZATION FLYWHEEL

Church - Missionaries - Gathering Framework

Every person needs a healthy, biblical church family. Every believer is called and empowered to be an "everyday missionary." Gatherings can become new churches, strengthen existing churches or multiply themselves.

Additional Made for More Resources

Exponential and Made for More put together a large library of FREE Resources to go along with the 2019 theme Made for More: Mobilizing God's People, God's Way.

Additional Made for More Resources
- eBooks
    - *Made for More Bible Study*
    - *Made for More Devotional*
    - *Made for More Visual Guide*
    - *Millennials Calling*
    - *The Flywheel of Mobilization*
    - *Church Different*
    - More eBooks Coming!

- Made for More Resource Kits
    - Made for More Staff and Leadership Resource Kit
    - Made for More Personal Calling Kit

- Made for More On-Line Course

- Articles & Blog Posts (A collection of blog posts on Mobilizing God's People, God's Way.)

- Video Training (An exclusive video teaching series on how you can help mobilize every Christian into their calling to make disciples where they live, work, learn and play.)

- Audio Podcasts (a series of compelling conversations with some of today's most trusted voices on their personal calling.)

- Made for More Assessment Tool (coming soon!)

For information about the 2019 Made for More theme and other FREE Made for More Resources, please visit our Made for More Resource Page.

INSIDE

Acknowledgements

For my mom,
Without your undying love and
unwavering support, this book wouldn't exist.

Introduction

As believers, we are given an extraordinary opportunity to change the world for Christ. In His wisdom, God has blessed us with a "made for more" abundant life and He wants us to experience fullness and seize every blessing and opportunity available. Jesus designed each one of us uniquely and desires us to live as beloved disciples who make disciples. He sends us out to carry the gospel into every nook and cranny of our world.

This devotional originated from prayer, and I couldn't be more excited to share this time with you. For the last five years I've been studying biblical Greek. Paul's letter to the Ephesians is a masterwork of stunning richness and depth. My prayer for you is that as you walk through each of these daily devotions, you'll grow in faith and be encouraged to help others either enter into relationship with Jesus or deepen that relationship.

The book can be used for individual meditation or in weekly discussions with a group. It's divided into six chapters which include five devotions and one "Shift Work" section. These six Shift Work sections are designed to help you delve deeper into your spiritual journey and apply the principles to your life. Keep a journal or notebook handy so you can answer the questions and record insights. As disciples of Christ, we're instructed to constantly learn, grow and change to be more like Him.

Each weekly Shift is based on a chapter in Ephesians and comes directly from the book *Made For More: Six Essential Shifts for Creating a Culture of Mobilization*. While the book and these six shifts were written specifically to church leaders, we can still use them to help us make critical changes as we discover God's design for His Church and His design for our individual lives. Because, after all, we *are* the Church. The six shifts include:

Ephesians 1 – From More Effort . . . to More Jesus

Ephesians 2 – From More Volunteers . . . to More Masterpieces

Ephesians 3 – From More Guilt . . . to More Love

Ephesians 4 – From More Hierarchy . . . to More Missionaries

Ephesians 5 – From More Programs . . . to More Mission Fields

Ephesians 6 – From More Strategy . . . to More Surrender

In Christ, we find peace, personal fulfillment and joy. When we serve out of a deep love for Him and His people, we grow in strength and maturity. Ultimately, Ephesians is infused with and immersed in love. Did you know that in this one letter alone, Paul uses the word and its iterations (loved, loving, beloved, etc.) more than fifteen times?

We grow in our faith and follow His calling on our lives only through love. As Paul reminds us in his first letter to the Corinthians, without love we gain nothing. Listen to his words: *If I speak in the tongues of men or of angels, but do not have love, I am only a resounding gong or a clanging cymbal. If I have the gift of prophecy and can fathom all mysteries and all knowledge, and if I have faith that can move mountains, but do not have love, I am nothing. If I give all I possess to the poor and give over my body to hardship that I may boast, but do not have love, I gain nothing* (1 Cor. 13:1-3).

Thank you for downloading this eBook. May you grow in your love for our Savior as you discover how He has made you for so much more.

Week One

FROM MORE EFFORT ...
TO MORE JESUS

Week One - Day One

ILLUMINATING THE MYSTERY OF MORE

Blessed be the God and Father of our Lord Jesus Christ,
who has blessed us in Christ with every spiritual
blessing in the heavenly places (Eph. 1:3).

We're able to see only a fraction of the stars and planets in our galaxy. Though people have tried, there are just too many to count. According to astronomers at *Sky and Telescope* magazine, roughly 9,000 stars can be viewed with the naked eye.

That number gets cut in half depending on atmospheric conditions, seasons and light pollution. The average New York City resident sees just seven stars, but the view for desert dwellers is vastly different.

However, viewing the stars and planets through binoculars and telescopes exponentially increases our abilities to see them. Trillions of galaxies illuminate the heavens and enable us to see the universe in an entirely new way.

As the creator of the earth, God has given us land and waters swarming with creatures and new species are constantly being discovered. The heavens, or what we call "outer space," are completely filled with cosmic wonder. Constellations map out the sky and meteor showers put on dazzling light shows. This is how big our God is!

In the same way a loving parent creates a healthy and happy home, our Creator has provided the perfect environment for us out of His boundless love for us. We are a blessed people—children of the divine creator of the universe. A God who is so big he literally fills everything.

But He doesn't stop with earthly blessings. He has also given us access to unimaginable spiritual blessings. Scripture tells us that we have access to *every kind of blessing* available. They originate from an unlimited and infinite God—given to us through Jesus.

In Christ, we discover we're made for more than what we can imagine.

Our Heavenly Father who created the stars and breathes life into every living thing has mind-blowing things in store for us, His children—when we're open to discovery. Like the stars in the sky, He designed each one of us uniquely for His great purposes. He has called us to illuminate our world for Christ and build up His body, the Church–to illuminate the mystery of more for ourselves and for others.

And here's the really big idea: the Church is called for more because Jesus Himself is more. Look at what Paul says about Jesus in Ephesians 1:22:

"God placed all things under Jesus' feet."

Only Jesus can fill everything in every way. Not our efforts, our strategies, our plans, our spouses, our children, our jobs, our church.

Only Jesus.

How does knowing that you have access to every kind of spiritual blessing expand your knowledge of and love for God?

Week One - Day Two

CHOSEN

He chose us in him before the foundation of the world, that
we should be holy and blameless before him (Eph. 1:4).

As a kid, I wasn't chosen for much of anything. There's not an athletic bone in my body, so when it came time to pick teams in school, I was on the sidelines until the bitter end. Even in the things I did well (like spelling), teachers didn't call on me often unless I frantically raised my hand. If I'm honest, those experiences undermined my confidence and made me feel insignificant.

I didn't grow up knowing God. In fact, in my home Christ wasn't mentioned in a positive way. Instead, I was raised to believe that hard work and self-determination were the pathways to success. I focused all my energy on making something of myself. Perhaps you can relate.

It wasn't until I was in my early twenties after my father died that I began searching for Jesus. And let me tell you, it wasn't an easy process. I had no one in my life to explain who Jesus was and all He had done. But God is faithful.

Let me pause here for a supernatural story. Though I didn't have knowledge about God, I always believed there was a powerful force in the universe. When I was little, my great grandmother sent me some prayers in the mail. I'd memorized this popular bedtime one: "Now I lay me down to sleep, I pray the Lord my soul to keep. If I should die before I wake, I pray the Lord my soul to take. That was the extent of my God knowledge, and I said the prayer every night, just in case."

The night of my father's funeral, our family and close friends were gathered around the dining room table reminiscing about my dad. I asked them, "Where is he now?" No one could answer, and I was beside myself in grief and anger. I wanted so desperately to believe in Heaven; I wanted to know I'd see him again one day. In the silence of the room, I heard a voice in my head (not my voice) say, "Go find Jesus, and He'll tell you where he is."

There's more to the story of course, but that voice sent me seeking. The Jesus i found met me in my grief and set me on the path of a new life.

It took a while to start reading the Bible. At first, I didn't understand a thing in it. But hard work and determination paid off. Reading small sections of

Scripture each day increased my knowledge and helped me make sense of my new spiritual life.

One verse, in particular, flipped my world upside down: *"You did not choose me, but I chose you and appointed you so that you might go and bear fruit–fruit that will last–and so that whatever you ask in my name the Father will give you"* (John 15:16).

Jesus' words washed over me. All these years of thinking I was the seeker... when I wasn't the seeker at all. *God* was. He was the One guiding me toward Him. I hadn't "chosen" Jesus; He had chosen me.

He has chosen you, too.

In Ephesians 1:4, Paul tells us we were chosen in Him before God formed the earth. Let that sink in. As His Church, we are chosen by Jesus to carry Christ's fullness into every corner of culture and sphere of society. The Church is the people of God saved by the power of God for the purposes of God. It is all the people of God on everyday mission to fill everything in every way with the fullness of Jesus.

What a relief it is to know that though we still work hard, we don't need to strive to make something of ourselves. He is the ultimate maker, and He wants so much more for us, His Church.

How does it feel knowing God chose you for His team?

Week One - Day Three

ENLIGHTENED

I do not cease to give thanks for you, remembering you in my prayers, that the God of our Lord Jesus Christ, the Father of glory, may give you the Spirit of wisdom and of revelation in the knowledge of him, having the eyes of your hearts enlightened, that you may know what is the hope to which he has called you, what are the riches of his glorious inheritance in the saints, and what is the immeasurable greatness of his power toward us who believe according to the working of his great might that he worked in Christ (Eph. 1:16-19).

In the eighteenth century, a flame burned across Europe and changed the course of world history. It's a period known as "The Enlightenment" or the "Age of Reason." Historians say it was a time of intellectual and philosophical growth in which reason reigned supreme as the basis for all legitimate thought.

Innovative ideas in the areas of scientific understanding and individual liberty sparked political change and, in some cases, revolution. Much of what we think today is influenced by this time period. For example, the ideas of democracy, personal rights to liberty and property. As with any movement, The Enlightenment had its pros and cons, but the end result was lasting impact.

In many ways, enlightenment looks like a spotlight being shined in darkness, fully exposing something you have never seen. This is what Paul wanted us to experience when he wrote, "...having the eyes of your hearts enlightened." He goes on to say that he wants us to open the eyes of our hearts so we fully know God.

Paul reminds us that God's end goal for His Church (remember the Church is the people of God saved by the power of God for the purposes of God) is knowledge and revelation of Him—anticipating that we'll understand the height and depth of the *hope* we're called to; the *riches* of what we've inherited in Him; and the unfathomable *power* accessible to us. Let's look at these three gifts more closely.

Hope, as defined in the Greek, is "looking forward with confidence to that which is good and beneficial." This isn't the same as wishing for something, but knowing in the depths of our soul that God's Word is true and He keeps His promises. We look forward with confidence.

Many of us today don't expect to inherit much of anything from our earthly parents, but we do have an inheritance stored up in Heaven. The theme of inheritance runs throughout the Old and New Testaments. Let's look at three scriptures from the Gospel of Matthew–these words come from Jesus Himself:

Blessed are the meek, for they will inherit the earth (v. 5:5);

And everyone who has left houses or brothers or sisters or father or mother or wife or children or fields for my sake will receive a hundred times as much and will inherit eternal life" (v. 19:29);

Then the King will say to those on his right, Come you who are blessed by my Father; take your inheritance, the kingdom prepared for you since the creation of the world" (v. 25:34).

We serve the God of Heaven who appointed us a Savior, Jesus, and raised Him from the dead. His power toward us is immeasurable, and He wants us to know and understand the full extent of it. Multiple lifetimes of exploration wouldn't begin to touch on the magnitude of this power.

We are not without resources. God gives us His Word for instruction and application. Entering into a personal relationship with His Son is the first key to unlocking understanding. Colossians 1:15 tells us: *The Son is the image of the invisible God, the firstborn over all creation.*

When we follow Him, we're spiritually illuminated, and our destiny is discipleship.

Revolution isn't possible until we change the way we think about Jesus.

What keeps you from seeing the hope you are called to, the riches of your inheritance and the power you have access to?

Week One - Day Four

ADOPTED

In love he predestined us for adoption to himself as sons through Jesus Christ, according to the purpose of his will (Eph. 1:5).

In New Testament times, adoption was practiced in a way that differs from our modern method. Learning about it greatly enhances our understanding of this scripture.

According to *Nelson's New Illustrated Bible Dictionary*, "Roman law required that the adopter be a male and childless; the one to be adopted had to be an independent adult, able to agree to be adopted. In the eyes of the law, the adopted one became a new creature; he was regarded as being born again into the new family."

In God's great love, through Jesus, we are adopted into God's family. We are His sons and daughters! This alone is an undeniable gift, but when we read through the first chapter of Ephesians, we learn there's more… much more:

Everything given to Jesus is transferred to us.

God clearly has a will, purpose and plan for our lives that begins with a new identity. The first chapter of Ephesians gives us a list of all we gain:

We have every spiritual blessing (v. 3).

We're chosen (v. 4).

We're His children (v. 5).

We're redeemed (v. 7).

We're forgiven (v. 7).

We're part of His purpose for the world (v. 9).

We've obtained an inheritance (v. 11).

We're sealed with the Holy Spirit (v. 13).

That list takes my breath away. I encourage you to read through it again and really think about what each one means and how it plays out in your life.

We may never be rich in this life, but we're loaded in Christ!

No wonder Paul was such a grateful guy. He was painfully aware of his own sin and putrid past (check out his story in Acts 9:1-31). Paul never forgot where he came from and who he'd been before meeting Jesus, but (and this is an important but), he also never dwelled there.

He was changed from a slaughterer to a son. He was called to be more, and so are we.

Christ has adopted you as His child. How does that change how you see Him and yourself?

Week One - Day Five

FILLED

And he put all things under his feet and gave him as
head over all things to the church, which is his body, the
fullness of him, who fills all in all (Eph. 1:22-23).

One of the hottest toys in the '80s was called Shrinky Dinks. They were thin sheets of plastic that could be colored and cut into shapes. Then they were placed on a baking sheet in a hot oven. Presto! In a few minutes, they would shrink down into thick little plastic pieces. We'd turn them into charms or tiny toys to trade with friends.

The only downside was that an adult needed to supervise the baking, although I will admit to breaking that rule. What can I say? I was hooked on them. In addition to being fun, I found they magically made me popular at school. I'd fill my pockets and use them to win friends and influence people.

But novelties wear off; newer and hotter things emerge on the market, and we turn our attention elsewhere. Back then, a popular saying was, "He who dies with the most toys wins."

Have you ever been guilty of treating God this way? We shrink Him down in our minds or take Him out when we're trying to get something. We use Him as a lucky charm or as a way to win people, and cast Him aside when our scheme doesn't work.

Trying to reduce God to make Him fit into our preconceived notions or plans is a colossal mistake. There is no minimizing Him. He's everything. He's too powerful to be manipulated or confined to the limitations of our human brains. Our inadequate presumptions certainly don't change who God is. On the contrary, they make us utterly ineffective.

Pastor and author Rob Wegner refers to this attempt to reduce Jesus to fit our ideas or lifestyle as "Little Jesus" syndrome. But just like God is too big to be confined by our imagination, there's nothing little about Jesus either.

He's so big that God put all things under His control—all things in Heaven, on earth and under the earth. He fills everything, everywhere, with the fullness of Him as the supreme ruler of the universe. Totality is expressed in the word "fullness" that Paul uses.

And the Church, as His body, is under the headship of Christ. He is our sovereign leader, not a Shrinky Dink savior. When we're in relationship with Him, He grows ever larger.

John the Baptist had the right perspective when he said, *"He must increase, but I must decrease"* (John 3:30).

What areas of your life reflect a "Little Jesus" syndrome? What keeps you from experiencing the fullness of Jesus?

Week One - Day Six

SHIFT WORK

Discipleship is an ongoing, ever-evolving process. "Shift Work" is about making critical changes towards spiritual growth. We continually mature in Christ and as we do, our old self–our natural sin-filled self–sloughs off.

The **First Shift** we need to make is to change the way we think about God and see Him everywhere we live, work, learn and play.

Read through these statements and questions and think about each one thoughtfully. In your journal or notebook, record any thoughts or scripture verses that speak to you.

Rob Wegner, teaching pastor at Westside Family Church in Kansas City, says, "As the Church, we should be obsessed with Jesus growing ever-larger in our minds and hearts." Eph 1:23

How obsessed with Jesus are you? Rate yourself on a scale of 1 - 5, with 5 being the most and 1 being the least:

What evidence would convict you of "being obsessed for Jesus"?
Kingdom minded all day long ...

Ephesians 1:3 tells us we're the recipients of **every** spiritual blessing in the heavenly places. Write down all the spiritual blessings you're aware of. glory to glory, being set free, loving people more

Jesus is more, and we are made for more. What areas of your life have more Jesus?
work, family, prayer life

In what areas of your life do you need more Jesus?

How well are you doing at revealing the fullness of Jesus in every sphere of your life?

Thus far, what's the biggest thing God has ever done for you?

When you think of Christ's Kingdom, what images come to mind?

The fullness of His glory with everyone praising Him

What's the thing you're most afraid to do when it comes to serving God and why?

If you could go anywhere in the world to serve Christ, where would it be and why? *I want to be where He wants me. I guess that means here, now.*

Week Two

FROM MORE VOLUNTEERS ... TO MORE MASTERPIECES

Week Two - Day One

DEAD

And you were dead in the trespasses and sins in which you once walked, following the course of this world, following the prince of the power of the air, the spirit that is now at work in the sons of disobedience—among whom we all once lived in the passions of our flesh, carrying out the desires of the body and the mind, and were by nature children of wrath, like the rest of mankind (Eph. 2:1-3).

Every year around Halloween, locals in our community gather for a Zombie Walk to raise money for the city food bank. Adults and children wear ripped clothing as costumes and paint their bodies to look like the undead. It's a lighthearted event for a good cause, especially since zombies are just fiction.

Still, I wonder if the idea of being among the walking dead is so far-fetched. If you look at Scripture, God has a lot to say to us about being spiritually dead.

In his letter to the Romans, the apostle Paul explains that sin separates us from God and reminds you and me that we were once dead in our trespasses and sins. God's Word is the standard for upright hearts, pure motives and appropriate conduct. Sin is missing the mark of that standard and drives a wedge in our relationship with Him. But God loved us so much that He freely gave us His Son so that we wouldn't remain spiritually dead.

Romans 6:23 tells us: *For the wages of sin is death, but the free gift of God is eternal life in Christ Jesus our Lord.*

Because of what Jesus did for us and our acceptance of Him as Lord and Savior, we're no longer separated. We have been raised to life with Christ.

Still, zombies are all around us.

Lost and wayward children who don't yet know Jesus as their Savior are found in every sphere of society--where we live, work, learn and play. Like us, these souls matter greatly to God. They don't understand what it means to be spiritually dead because they don't know the One who gives life. But we do because we were once like these spiritually dead souls.

Every follower of Jesus is called to make disciples. He has created each one of us as a unique masterpiece and has given us a mission field. He has called us to continue in Jesus' work of seeking and saving the lost.

Now it's time to think outside the box. What creative strategies and tactics could you use to begin a relationship with the spiritually dead where you live, work, learn and play?

Week Two - Day Two

SAVED

*For by grace you have been saved through faith. And this
is not your own doing; it is the gift of God, not a result
of works, so that no one may boast* (Eph. 2:8-9).

Do you know people who like to be in control? Someone who needs to have their hand in everything, everywhere, at all times? Maybe that's you or a spouse, boss or parent in your life.

We can agree that for the most part, people who have a "my way or the highway" attitude are annoying. Without delving too deeply into motivations and mindset, there are several reasons we can be prone to this behavior. Feelings of insecurity, the need for affirmation, and a conceited attitude are some of the many possible causes.

I believe Paul had deep insight into our human tendency to want to be in control. He wanted his hearers to know that the grace through which they had been saved had *absolutely nothing* to do with them, their effort or accomplishment. He first makes the statement, *"For by grace you have been saved through faith"* and then reinforces it with a threefold response:

- Grace is not deserved or your own doing.

- It's a gift of God--nothing you did made it happen.

- You can't take credit for it.

Simply defined, grace is undeserved kindness. It is a gift.

The Bible tells us that our faith is also a gift: *For by the grace given me I say to everyone of you: Do not think of yourself more highly than you ought, but rather think of yourself with sober judgment, in accordance with the measure of faith God has given you* (Rom. 12:3).

Paul knew a thing or two about arrogance and conceit. He was well-known for being a persecutor of Christians, that is, until Jesus literally knocked him off his high horse.

Grace and faith work hand-in-hand as miracle activators. In just one of many healing stories, Matthew recounts the tale of two blind men who came to Jesus hoping for restored sight. He first asked them, *"Do you believe that I am able to do this?"* After they said they did, He touched their eyes and said, *"According to your faith will it be done to you,"* and their sight was restored (Matt. 9:28-29).

The bottom line is that all we have and all we are is a gift from God.

And here's the kicker. God gave us these gifts of grace and faith to be shared with others—not to just keep for ourselves. When we share our faith and extend grace, we're reminded of our humble status before God. We also get to participate in the miracle-working process!

How can you share the gifts of grace and faith with the people you see and engage with today?

Week Two - Day Three

ALL ACCESS

*And he came and preached peace to you who were far off
and peace to those who were near. For through him we both
have access in one Spirit to the Father* (Eph. 2:17-18).

Last year for my husband's birthday, I bought us tickets to a show in Las Vegas. I wanted him to have the fullest experience possible, so I purchased an All Access Pass, which included front-row seating and backstage passes. After the show, I asked if he wanted to go back and meet the performers.

Surprisingly, he told me, "No, I wouldn't even know what to say." Instead of taking full advantage of our passes, we left the theater as others lined up behind velvet ropes to meet the cast.

In Ephesians 2:17-18, Jesus is the preacher of peace Paul is writing about. Paul says Jesus brought His Good News to two different groups of people: those who were near (the Jews) and those far off (the Gentiles). Essentially, Paul tells us that message is for all of us ... that we have full access to our Creator and Savior.

Through Jesus' sacrifice, we have access to our Heavenly Father who is not hidden behind a silky curtain or velvet ropes. He doesn't show partiality to those in the front-row seats because all who believe in Him are welcome. All have full access to His throne of grace.

The original Greek word Paul used for "access" is *prosagoge* (pronounced pros-a-go-gay). It's defined as the right or opportunity to address someone, implying that the person who is addressed has a higher status. This is part of the profound mystery of God. We, who are mere mortals, have access to the Creator of the universe through His Son.

It's one of the many spiritual blessings believers enjoy and others have yet to experience. Just imagine for a minute what the world would be like without Him. Maybe remember a time when you were "far off" and someone told you about the gospel of peace.

What stops us from sharing this truth with others? Fear? Doubt?

One of Jesus' own disciples struggled with doubt. His disbelief even earned him a nickname. When Jesus told His followers that He was going to be with His

Father, He reassured them that He'd come back one day and take all of them to be with Him.

But that wasn't enough for Thomas, who asked Jesus, *"Lord, we do not know where you are going. How can we know the way?"* (John 14:5).

In His response, Jesus gave us (and Doubting Thomas) a profound promise and helped us understand just who He is and the gift of full access He brings: *"I am the way, and the truth, and the life. No one comes to the Father except through me"* (John 14:6).

Do you live as if you have full access to your Creator and Savior? Who in your sphere is far off and desperately needs to know they have full access to Jesus and His message of peace?

Week Two - Day Four

SACRIFICE

*But now in Christ Jesus you who once were far off have
been brought near by the blood of Christ* (Eph 2:13).

One of my friends tells a hilarious story about the birth of her first child. She and her husband were, like most parents, thrilled to learn about her pregnancy. They got ready for the birth by taking parenting classes, practicing breathing exercises and touring the hospital. When the great day came, they felt ready. They had done everything they could to be prepared for the amazing event.

She got to the hospital in a fairly advanced stage of labor, and the nurses got her settled in a delivery suite. Her husband (a burly man's man) waited by her side the whole time and held her hand through powerful contractions. The nurse tried inserting an IV into my friend's vein and a tiny drop of blood appeared. One glance, and her hubby fell to the floor in a heap as the nurse yelled, "Man down!" He watched his wife give birth from a chair at her bedside.

Blood makes some people squeamish, but it was a common sight in ancient times–especially for those living in the Roman Empire. Public whipping and crucifixion were routine forms of punishment for criminals. Blood rituals were used in magic, and the Jews sacrificed substitutionary animals to atone for sin.

The ancients viewed sacrificial blood as having strengthening and cleansing properties. A multitude of scriptures about Christ's blood run through the New Testament. Hebrews 10:19 gives us clarity about its power:

*Therefore, brothers, since we have confidence to enter the holy places by the blood
of Jesus, by the new and living way that He opened for us through the curtain,
that is, through His flesh, and since we have a great priest over the house of God,
let us draw near with a true heart in full assurance of faith, with our hearts
sprinkled clean from an evil conscience and our bodies washed with pure water.
Let us hold fast the confession of our hope without wavering, for He who promised
is faithful.*

Jesus' work on the cross is the pre-eminent event of world history. Without His sacrifice, we would all be destined for destruction. His death broke down the barrier between God and humanity, and He's seated in Heaven as our great high priest. Our work for Jesus also requires a yielding of ourselves for His purpose.

What can you sacrifice to draw others near or nearer to Christ?

Week Two - Day Five

UNITED

For He Himself is our peace, who has made us both one and has broken down in His flesh the dividing wall of hostility by abolishing the law of commandments expressed in ordinances, that He might create in himself one new man in place of the two, so making peace, and might reconcile us both to God in one body through the cross, thereby killing the hostility (Eph. 2:14-16).

The United States Supreme Court is a group of nine men and women making decisions on some of the most important legal cases in our nation's history. Though each Justice is an individual, they work in unison as one body.

Despite the unique circumstances of their confirmation processes, political leanings and personal dispositions, these nine leaders come together to make decisions that affect individuals and the country as a whole.

Recently, I learned about one of their many interesting traditions. "The Judicial Handshake" dates back to the nineteenth century. Each day before they go on the bench and before any discussion in private conferences, they gather together and shake hands with each of their counterparts.

According to the Supreme Court website, there's a reason for this: "Chief Justice Fuller instituted this practice as a reminder that differences of opinion on the Court did not preclude overall harmony of purpose."

As believers, we're also called to unity—to be one as the body of Christ. The "broken down" reference in our daily verse above is mild compared to what it actually means, which is total destruction. The hostility that formerly divided people and made them enemies suffered total devastation when Jesus willingly chose to die on the cross for us.

His purpose of making peace through reconciliation offers us a clear pattern to follow. By His example, we as His disciples are called to do the same in the here and now. We have a ministry of reconciliation.

As Ephesians 2:22 tells us: *In him you also are being built together into a dwelling place for God by the Spirit.*

Think about that. While much of the world is divided and dominated by hostility and enmity, a bright light still shines—us. Citizens and family members have rights and responsibilities to their leaders and relatives. Putting hostility and individuality aside for the sake of others is critical for any healthy household.

Jesus accomplished this for us on the cross. He calls us to pick up our cross—our responsibility—and to follow Him.

Is there anyone you need to make peace with and be reconciled to? How can you live more united?

Week Two - Day Six

SHIFT WORK

Discipleship is an ongoing, ever-evolving process. "Shift Work" is about making critical changes towards spiritual growth. We continually mature in Christ and, as we do, our old self–our natural sin-filled self–sloughs off.

The **Second Shift** we need to make is to investigate and discover the unique ways in which God designed us.

Read through these statements and questions and think thoughtfully about each one. In your journal or notebook, record any thoughts or Scripture that speak to you.

For we are His workmanship, created in Christ Jesus for good works, which God prepared beforehand, that we should walk in them (Eph. 2:10).

Jesus is the master designer and has made each one of us a unique masterpiece. We are responsible for doing good works in service and discovering the unique qualities He has given us for this purpose. Reflect on the questions below to begin to unveil the picture God is creating.

What do you think you're good at? *listening, supporting, encouraging*

What do other people tell you you're good at? *good listener*

List five skills you've mastered. *making a plan, following through, remaining hopeful*

What causes or people groups do you care about? *Those in my life, others as God leads*

If you could do anything in the world, what would it be? *Be bolder in expressing my faith in words and actions*

What scripture verses compel or convict you to action? *Be not weary in well-doing*

What do you think God is calling you to do with your gifts? *Look for opportunities to use them daily*

What changes in your life are necessary to make this happen?

More time with God

Is a clear picture of your masterpiece life beginning to emerge?

If so, describe it and then share it with someone in your life.

If not, what could you do daily or regularly to help you start to see that picture or see it more clearly?

Week Three

FROM MORE GUILT ...
TO MORE LOVE

Week Three - Day One

PRISONER OF JESUS

*For this reason I, Paul, a prisoner of Christ Jesus on behalf of you
Gentiles—assuming that you have heard of the stewardship of God's
grace that was given to me for you, how the mystery was made known
to me by revelation, as I have written briefly. When you read this, you
can perceive my insight into the mystery of Christ . . .* (Eph. 3:1-2).

What wouldn't you do for Jesus? Where wouldn't you go? Jesus stopped at nothing-- even giving up His life--to be obedient to His Father. And He gave this same command to us:

*Whoever serves me must follow me; and where I am, my servant also will be. My
Father will honor the one who serves me* (John 12:26).

Not many of us are willing to risk persecution for Jesus' sake, but Paul wrote Ephesians while under house arrest in Rome. In his words, I sense no attitude of self-pity or regret. Instead, his letters are filled with gratitude. Paul didn't let his personal circumstances and environment divert his commitment to making the gospel clear for the sake of others.

In fact, he considered his task a gift of grace and part of God's prearranged plan. No level of persecution could squelch his joy or stop him from doing what he knew the Lord had called him to do.

He also wrote a letter to the Philippians during this time in prison and encouraged them with these words: *I want you to know brothers, that what has happened to me has really served to advance the gospel, so that it has become known throughout the whole imperial guard and to all the rest that my imprisonment is for Christ. And most of the brothers, having become confident in the Lord by my imprisonment, are much more bold to speak the word without fear* (Phil. 1:12-14).

The Imperial Guard he references was made up of over 4,500 elite warriors. So not only did they hear about Jesus, believers were emboldened as well. Paul shows us that we can serve God wherever we are and in whatever circumstance because these external factors aren't barriers to discipleship. In fact, they may just serve to advance the gospel.

Maybe you feel imprisoned by a situation–an illness, financial hardship, work environment or a difficult marriage. Maybe you doubt you can benefit others when your life is topsy-turvy. Jesus has something to say about that. And His promise is timeless: *I will be with you wherever you go, even to the end of the age* (Matt. 28:20).

If you're leading others, I encourage you to reach out in love to those in difficult situations. I was housebound with an illness for almost two years with little help and no contact from local church leaders. You probably know many people with similar stories who want to serve in some way but feel forgotten. What an encouragement it is to know that God meets us in all our circumstances, even negative ones.

Where wouldn't you go for Jesus? Do any circumstances prevent you from serving?

Week Three - Day Two

CALLED

Of this gospel I was made a minister according to the gift of God's grace, which was given me by the working of his power (Eph. 3:7).

Twenty years ago, I attended a ministry worship night at my new church. A young mother at the time, I remember feeling extremely isolated and lonely. I'd never attended an event like this before, and I was nervous. But my longing for community and adult conversation outweighed my apprehension.

At the end of the evening, a new part-time children's minister introduced herself to all of us. Carol was looking for help. Because she didn't live locally (she was two states away), she was hoping to find someone to coordinate the people serving in the kid's ministry.

After her talk, Carol stood silently waiting while music played softly in the background. The discomfort of those in the room was palpable. After a few uncomfortable minutes passed, I raised my hand.

I don't know exactly what made me do it, but I thought if she could drive for four hours one way and leave her family every weekend, I could certainly make a few phone calls. After the service, we talked briefly and arranged to meet the next day for lunch. I didn't know what to expect, but it was too late to turn back.

The next day we met at a restaurant. She outlined her plan and said, "This is your ministry so I'm available to help and guide, but how you do it is up to you." We talked for a bit and before we ended the conversation, she said a prayer of encouragement and asked God to bless my ministry.

I was embarrassed and didn't want to let her down, but I needed clarity.

"Carol, I don't know what you mean when you say 'my ministry.' I'm just a volunteer making phone calls."

I still remember how full of grace she was toward me, new in my journey with Christ.

"Ministry is your area of service to God, and you'll be ministering to the adults who serve the kids," she explained. "You're more than a volunteer; you're a minister."

Carol's service and passion for God altered my life forever. I served first as a coordinator, then a teacher, a children's worship leader and eventually went into vocational children's ministry at that same church.

God's grace changed the trajectory of my life in every way, and I've since been able to help others understand and find their place in ministry. When you serve God, you're more than a volunteer. You're a Kingdom-building missionary.

Where do you serve? Do you think of yourself as a volunteer, or do you see yourself as more? A Kingdom builder? A missionary? Do you think of yourself as "called"?

Week Three - Day Three

CREATED

To me, though I am the very least of all the saints, this grace was given, to preach to the Gentiles the unsearchable riches of Christ, and to bring to light for everyone what is the plan of the mystery hidden for ages in God, who created all things, so that through the church the manifold wisdom of God might now be made known to the rulers and authorities in the heavenly places (Eph. 3:8-11).

I'm continually amazed by Paul and his confidence in his ministry mission. We know he was a humble man by reading what he wrote and the stories told about him. He always credited God's grace as the source of his success.

I often wish I was as self-assured and steadfast in my service to God, but sometimes I get wishy-washy about how I measure up. Yes, I know full well that comparing myself to others doesn't benefit anyone and actually hinders my work for the Kingdom. But admittedly, my zeal can get clouded by confusion and comments of others. Maybe you've experienced this, too.

As a child, one of my favorite school activities was doing dot-to-dots. The teacher would hand out papers with nothing on them but a series of numbered dots. We'd take our pencils and carefully connect the dots according to the numbers. Eventually, a picture would emerge. If correctly connected, an image of an animal or person would appear.

The hidden picture idea is a lot like our spiritual lives. We all have different circumstances, life events and people who come and go, seemingly at random. Sometimes, we ask God, *Why did I have to experience something so awful?* or *What's the point of this person being in my life?* The answers may be hidden for us then (sometimes forever), but they're no mystery to the one who created us.

Life is messy, but your experiences aren't like haphazard dots on a page (though they may often feel like it). Instead, they're carefully designed by a divine artist. Paul was God's perfect choice for His mission. His life *before* Jesus was preparation for his life *with* Jesus.

The same holds true for us. God's wisdom is manifold, which means multi-sided and diverse. And His wisdom gets activated through the Church (that's us) to bring light and make the mystery and message of Christ known to the world.

The completed picture, plan and purpose have always existed even if we can't quite see it. However, discovering our personal, unique calling requires us to get down to business and connect the dots. General calling and personal calling are different. In general, we're called to belief in and obedience to Jesus; to be disciples who make disciples. Personal calling is the unique way He has created us to achieve His purpose of bringing Christ to the world.

As he explains in his book, *More,* author Todd Wilson, says, "God's work in us isn't just rescuing us from the abyss . . . it's about being called to our destiny. He calls us to Himself to rediscover who we were created to be."

God has created a personal plan for your life and a calling uniquely designed by Him. Are you ready to connect the dots?

Week Three - Day Four

BOUNDLESS

For this reason I bow my knees before the Father, from whom every family in heaven and on earth is named, that according to the riches of his glory he may grant you to be strengthened with power through his Spirit in your inner being, so that Christ may dwell in your hearts through faith – that you, being rooted and grounded in love, may have strength to comprehend with all the saints what is the breadth and length and height and depth, and to know the love of Christ that surpasses knowledge, that you may be filled with all the fullness of God (Eph. 3:14-19).

In the third chapter of his letter to the church in Ephesus, Paul repeatedly reminds us that prayer is like a rocket launcher for our faith. In the same way the launcher propels a rocket into the air, prayer is our method for direct communication with the God of the universe.

The target for Paul's prayer in these verses is our inner being, our heart. In the ancient world, the word "heart" means our thoughts and mind. It encompasses our entire being. His multifaceted prayer is that through being rooted and grounded in love, we'd be filled with all the fullness of God.

Our inner being is the dwelling place of God. In his Gospel, John exhorts us: *Dear friends, let us continue to love one another, for love comes from God. Anyone who loves is a child of God and knows God. But anyone who does not love does not know God, for God is love* (John 4:7-8).

Our Savior's love for people is boundless; there's nowhere it doesn't reach. No height nor depth restrictions exist, and no boundary lines can't be crossed. The highest mountains, deepest oceans and worst criminals aren't beyond His reach.

In his message to Timothy, Paul makes this crystal clear: *I urge you, first of all, to pray for all people. Ask God to help them; intercede on their behalf, and give thanks for them. Pray this way for kings and all who are in authority so that we can live peaceful and quiet lives marked by godliness and dignity. This is good and pleases God our Savior, who wants everyone to be saved and to understand the truth. For there is only one God and one Mediator who can reconcile God and humanity—the man Christ Jesus. He gave his life to purchase freedom for everyone* (1 Tim. 2:1-6).

Our motivation for every aspect of discipleship must be rooted and grounded in the same infinite love Jesus has for us. Like He was sent to us, we are also "sent" to others.

Author Michael Frost says, "We are mobilized to fill everything everywhere with the fullness of Jesus. The resurrected Christ reminds us there is no place where we are not sent!"

If His love is boundless and He has "sent" us to go out into the world to make disciples, what are we waiting for?

How does knowing that God's love for you is boundless free you to go out into the world and serve?

Week Three - Day Five

UNIMAGINABLE

*Now to him who is able to do far more abundantly than all
that we ask or think, according to the power at work within us,
to him be glory in the church and in Christ Jesus throughout
all generations, forever and ever. Amen* (Eph. 3:20-21).

If you're a parent, you no doubt have beautiful dreams for your children. You want the best for them. Before our children are born, we imagine what they will physically look like and what it will feel like to hold them in our arms. As our babies grow, we start to wonder what they'll become and where they'll go—there's no limit to our imagination for our kids.

Of course at times, these beautiful beings inevitably disappoint us and do things we never thought they'd do. They go places they shouldn't go. And then sometimes, they knock our socks off and do far more than we ever thought they would. We get a glimpse of God's grand design for them and begin to realize who He created them to be.

When that happens, we do everything in our power to help them achieve their goals. We drive them to lessons, take them to practice and invest in their passion pursuits, knowing they'll be most fulfilled when using their God-given gifts and talents.

If only that kind of nurturing continued through the rest of their lives. Unfortunately as adults, the life-giving encouragement we once received as children gets pushed aside, especially in our local church, because someone needed to fill a slot. Instead of serving out of our personal calling and the design God has for us, we end up feeling frustrated and fatigued.

I remember when I moved away and joined a new church. I wanted to serve so I spoke with a leader. He asked me to work on the Communications Team helping design and put out the weekly newsletter. I explained that I knew nothing about graphics and absolutely hated working with computers.

"No problem," he said. "We'll train you."

Famous last words.

In short, it was a disaster. After several months, we both felt frustrated. He was too embarrassed to tell me how awful I was doing, and I resented him for not listening to me in the first place. Eventually, we called it quits and I went into the area of my gifting instead. In that place, the ministry and I both flourished.

Our Heavenly Father is the ultimate parent who knows in advance what we were meant to do. The plans He has are filled with unimaginable adventure and purpose. Our story is for His glory, and He has more in store for us than we can fathom.

Are you serving God using your unique giftings? Do you sense you're fulfilling God's design for your life? If not, what critical decisions do you need to make?

Week Three - Day Six

SHIFT WORK

The **Third Shift** we need to make helps us ensure that our service and leadership come from the motivation of loving God and loving people.

Read through these statements and questions and reflect on each one. In your journal or notebook, record any thoughts or scripture verses that speak to you.

Serving and leading are often difficult. It's easy to focus on the task and forget to love. Where do you find yourself?

Where are you currently serving?
Church, community

Do you feel you're in the right area? Why or why not?
yes in certain respects, questioning others

Who is supporting and encouraging you in your ministry and mission?
Out of comfort zone in fitness classes

Who can you support in their ministry and mission?
those whom I serve with

Using the dot-to-dot analogy on Day Three, list five dots in your life (skills, talents, circumstances, etc.) that point you toward your mission field.

How can you use those dots to serve God?

Share about a time God did something unimaginable in your area of ministry.

How does your church help move people into the "right-fit" ministry missions?

What shifts do you need to make to serve from love rather than obligation?

Find a "love" scripture in your Bible and write it out.

Week Four

FROM MORE HIERARCHY ...
TO MORE MISSIONARIES

Week Four - Day One

RECONCILED

I therefore, a prisoner for the Lord, urge you to walk in a manner worthy of the calling to which you have been called, with all humility and gentleness, with patience, bearing with one another in love, eager to maintain the unity of the Spirit in the bond of peace (Eph. 4:1-3).

Recent research suggests the worldwide Church is at a point of crisis. The global persecution of Christians is growing at an alarming rate, church attendance is down in the West, and the news is filled with stories about younger generations rejecting Christianity altogether.

Now is the time for us to come together as one family so that instead of the Church imploding, the Church begins exploding.

In Ephesians 4:1-3, Paul tells us we have been called to "live in a manner worthy of " that calling and gives us the keys to do that:

Humility and gentleness √

Patience and love √

Eagerness for unity √

These are characteristics, Paul says, that we should live out with one another and the world at large.

They're the distinguishing traits of Jesus who said, *"Come to me, all you who are weary and burdened, and I will give you rest. Take my yoke upon you and learn from me, for I am gentle and humble in heart and you will find rest for your souls. For my yoke is easy and my burden is light"* (Matt. 11:28-30).

In the Church, as in life, we can create and encounter problems because we're so busy working *for* Jesus that we forget to be *like* Jesus?

Our calling is a high and holy one. To walk in a way worthy of that calling, we must walk in the way of Christ. His way is loving and humble. Remember,

Jesus came to reconcile all things to Himself. This is the essence of unity and contains no divisions and strife.

Reconciliation is primary to God's plan. In fact, Paul reminds us of our obligation in 2 Corinthians 5:18-19: *All this is from God, who reconciled us to himself through Christ and gave us the ministry of reconciliation: that God was reconciling the world to himself in Christ, not counting people's sins against them. And he has committed to us the message of reconciliation.*

What do you need to change in your life to walk in a way worthy of God's plan to reconcile us to Him?

Week Four - Day Two

SERVED

There is one body and one Spirit – just as you were called to the one hope that belongs to your call – one Lord, one faith, one baptism, one God and Father of all, who is over all and through all and in all (Eph. 4:4-6).

In late August, Hurricane Florence barreled toward our small beach town causing mandatory evacuations. My family worked together to secure our home and gather up what little we could fit in one car. We drove to be with relatives in another state and watched the destruction on television. Because river flooding closed the highways, we weren't able to return home for three weeks.

During that time, we spent days scrolling through social media, looking at pictures and video of the devastation. One story in my news feed intrigued me— people everywhere posted warnings of "rafts" of fire ants floating on the surface of the water. Unfortunately, some folks learned about this freaky fact the hard way and got attacked by swarms.

The rafts were made up of hundreds of thousands of ants. The ant colony is impossible to destroy as long as its queen is alive. When the waters rose, they sprung into action and bonded together for one purpose: to protect the queen and her young. The frantic pace of this binding creates a structure that allows them to float and seek the safety of dry land.

Beneath the water, danger lurks as predators attempt to gobble them up and tear the raft apart. However, once the ants make it to land, they get back to work at building up their community.

I see so many parallels between this natural phenomenon and our faith. The survival of the fire ant community depends on their leader. The queen is their entire reason for being, and all they do centers around her. The strength of the ants' survival depends on them coming together as one unit for a critical purpose.

In the same way, Christ is building His Church (us) His way and wants all of us to join and serve in the communal effort He has designed and put into action. He is the One Lord, our leader, Savior and Master.

Paul tells us our call as Jesus' disciples carries with it a responsibility to serve. Faithful servants hear, obey and serve their Lord with all humility and love. This love extends itself toward Him and one another.

In Matthew's Gospel, Jesus reminds us of His purpose for coming to earth: *"The Son of Man did not come to be served, but to serve, and to give His life as a ransom for many"* (Matt. 20:2).

Have you ever thought of being someone God has served? How does knowing He first loved and served us impact how you serve with others in His mission?

Week Four - Day Three

GIFTED

But grace was given to each one of us according to the measure of Christ's gift. Therefore it says, "When He ascended on high He led a host of captives, and He gave gifts to men" (Eph. 4:7-8).

I'm the parent of three gifted children; two are artists, and one is a computer whiz. They're all smarter than their parents! Throughout today's culture, gifted people are all around. We're entertained by top-notch performers. We learn from teachers who clarify and impart knowledge; and our way of life is enhanced by inventive problem solvers.

What may be surprising to know is that we're all gifted in one way or another. Do you see yourself in this way?

The priceless gift of grace was measured out to each one of us through Jesus. Many scholars believe that Psalm 68:18 is an Old Testament prophetic scripture that refers to Christ:

When you ascended on high, you led captives in your train; you received gifts from men, even from the rebellious – that you, O Lord God, might dwell there.

Jesus is the ultimate victor who conquered Satan, sin and death. In ancient times, kings would invade a territory and capture people, including the nobility of the royal households he conquered. The king would march back his captives to his land and parade them in a "train" as a display of victory for his people to see.

In contrast, Christ took His own "prisoners of war," those captives whose hearts He conquered, and gave them to His people as gifts. We see in the Apostle Paul the perfect irony of this vivid imagery. As Saul, he persecuted Jesus followers and was on his way to Damascus to arrest and take Christians back to Jerusalem as his captives.

But something happened along the way and instead of capturing, Saul was captured. Jesus then gave him back to us as a gift–an apostle for the purpose of preaching to the Gentiles and building up His Church. Thereafter, in several letters to the churches he planted, Paul identified himself according to who he was in Christ: a servant of Christ Jesus; an apostle of Christ Jesus; a slave of Christ; and a prisoner for the Lord.

Well aware of *whose* He was, Paul fulfilled his work for the Kingdom in love and gratitude for the One who had transformed his life. He used his life as a gift and poured himself out on behalf of others. Throughout his ministry, he exhorts us to do the same.

Paul often urged people to follow his way of life, and this is a reminder of encouragement for us: *In everything I did, I showed you that by this kind of hard work we must help the weak, remembering the words the Lord Jesus Himself said: "It is more blessed to give than to receive"* (Acts 20:35).

We're gifted because of Christ's grace, and when we use those gifts of service for His Kingdom, the Church grows in maturity and numbers. The Church is all the people of God on everyday mission that fills everything everywhere with the fullness of Jesus.

What gifts can you identify and use to fulfill your everyday mission?

Week Four - Day Four

RENEWED

You, however, did not come to know Christ that way. Surely you heard of him and were taught in him in accordance with the truth that is in Jesus. You were taught, with regard to your former way of life, to put off your old self, which is being corrupted by its deceitful desires; to be made new in the attitude of your minds; and to put on the new self, created to be like God in true righteousness and holiness (Eph. 4:20-24).

Have you ever seen the TV show *Hoarders*? It's about people with hoarding disorder (a true mental illness) who collect and store things with disastrous results. Most often, their homes are stacked to the rafters. Worthless trash fills entire rooms, floors buckle under pressure, and in extreme cases rodents scavenge freely.

There's no order in a hoarder's world. Relationships are broken (if not completely destroyed), and quality of life is in the pits. Yet these people can't let go because their perspective is skewed. They can't release their "valuables"even if the purging will bring them reconciliation with loved ones and a better way of life. Again, it's a sickness. A psychiatrist and trash removal service are on hand to help remove the junk and begin the healing process.

Just as hoarders hang on to stuff, we can also hang on to junk that threatens to destroy. Sin, unhealthy thoughts and unholy relationships contaminate our spirit. To begin the heart renewal Jesus died for and put on our "new self," we first need to make space by clearing out the old.

If anyone could speak about life renewed, it was Paul. Meeting Jesus on the road to Damascus and throwing off his "old self" literally changed him--and the world.

We get a glimpse of Paul's life change in his words to Timothy: *I thank Christ Jesus our Lord, who has given me strength, that he considered me faithful, appointing me to his service. Even though I was once a blasphemer and a persecutor and a violent man, I was shown mercy because I acted in ignorance and unbelief. The grace of our Lord was poured out on me abundantly, along with the faith and love that are in Christ Jesus* (1 Tim. 1:12-14).

The truth is in Jesus. In fact, the truth *is* Jesus. Scripture tells us we are works in progress, never complete, and always moving toward righteousness and holiness through Him. Our journey is long and arduous, but Jesus supplies us with abundant strength and nourishment for our souls.

Jesus desires to give us full life in Him. He wants us to experience His love and join Him in the adventure He has in store for each one of us. But we need to be awake and alert. Sin separates us from God. So we must be diligent about cleaning house. Let's not hold on to the worthless clutter that belongs to the old way and robs us of the peace and joy a renewed heart brings.

As Jesus reminds us in John 10:10: *The thief comes only to steal and kill and destroy; I have come that they may have life, and have it to the full.*

What is the worthless junk you can begin tossing out to experience renewal of your heart and mind?

Week Four - Day Five

ATTACHED

It was He who gave some to be apostles, some to be prophets, some to be evangelists, and some to be pastors and teachers, to prepare God's people for works of service, so that the body of Christ may be built up until we all reach unity in the faith and in the knowledge of the Son of God and become mature, attaining to the whole measure of the fullness in Christ (Eph. 4:11-13).

Paul tells us that God's Church is organized for fullness. One look at his (very) long sentence in the passage above explains the how and why of the organizational structure. In ministry, the acronym for this fivefold structure is known as APEST, which stands for Apostles, Prophets, Evangelists, Shepherds and Teachers.

In their book, *Made for More: Six Essential Shifts for Creating a Culture of Mobilization*, authors Todd Wilson and Rob Wegner break down the functional strengths of these types of servants:

- **Apostle** - Pioneering, sending, extending, and entrepreneurial.

- **Prophet** - Questioning systems of power, seeking justice, critiquing mission drift and protecting the marginalized

- **Evangelist** - Reaching out, including the seeker, proclaiming the gospel and including new people

- **Shepherd** - Nurture, care, community and health

- **Teacher** - Sound doctrine, clear teaching, effective processes and systems, and strong values

Do you recognize any of these strengths in yourself?

Most of us aren't called into vocational ministry and will never be. Instead, we serve in all the areas where we live, work, learn and play. But as Ephesians 4:11-13 reminds us, we all have a part to play in building up the body of Christ. Our leaders are there to help us, the saints, prepare for service.

Author and teacher Alan Hirsch often talks and writes about APEST, focusing heavily on the Apostle gifting. Listen to what he says about the expression of Jesus in the world and our part in that: "Play with the image of body for awhile. The body is the embodiment. The German evangelist Dietrich Bonhoeffer said, 'The Church is the one place in the world where Jesus Christ is taking form.'

Hirsch continues: "It's not happening anywhere else. He has chosen this particular people to become the concrete expression of who He is, attached to Him as our Lord and the One who guides us."

We are attached to Christ who has organized us to both mature us and bring us into the fullness of Him.

How are you living into your spiritual gifting? How does knowing you're attached to Jesus help you live filled up and poured out to others?

Week Four - Day Six

SHIFT WORK

The **Fourth Shift** we need to make to live life to the fullest measure is to get rid of the junk that hinders our service and get serious about discovering and using our spiritual gifts.

Read through these statements and questions and think about each one thoughtfully. In your journal or notebook, record any thoughts or scripture verses that speak to you.

Paul talks about walking worthy of Christ. In your own words define the word "worthy."

Looking at the three characteristic clusters Paul mentioned–humility and gentleness; patience and love: and eagerness for unity–which (if any) values do you struggle with?

What shifts do you need to make in your life to adopt these values?

You have been gifted by God! List one or two of your spiritual gifts.

How might you use these gifts to serve Christ and His kingdom?

What would it look like to live your life to the fullest measure?

We all have to "clean house" from time to time and get rid of the old stuff that hinders us from putting on the "new self." What hindrances need to be trashed in your life?

Using the APEST model as an example, which ministry strength(s) best describes you? Do you see yourself as one of the five … because you are?

Week Five

FROM MORE PROGRAMS ...
TO MORE MISSION FIELDS

Week Five - Day One

FRAGRANCE

*Be imitators of God, therefore, as dearly loved children and live
a life of love, just as Christ loved us and gave Himself up for
us as a fragrant offering and sacrifice to God* (Eph 5:1-2).

In certain cultures, fragrance plays an important role in everyday life. My husband is from the Holy Land, and I experience this directly every day. Each morning after his shower, he "showers" again with cologne. He douses himself with it.

I'm talking head-to-toe spritzing. The fragrance is so strong that I can't go into the bathroom until it dissipates. It's become a running joke in our family that when we can't figure out what to buy him for a special occasion, we'll never go wrong with cologne.

In Scripture, One of the most known stories about fragrance in the Bible is the beautiful story of Mary, one of Jesus' disciples. I can just see this young woman carrying in a beautiful, translucent white alabaster jar filled with nard, a potent anointing oil and then, to everyone's surprise, she breaks the jar and pours out the fragrant offering on Jesus' head. The disciples there couldn't believe their eyes. Nard was used only for special occasions and instead of seeing the spiritual significance of her actions, they yelled at her for wasting what could have been sold and given to the poor.

I love Jesus' response and the way He stood up for Mary. He rebuked them, saying, *"Why are you bothering this woman? She has done a beautiful thing to me. The poor you will always have with you, but you will not always have me. When she poured this perfume on my body, she did it to prepare me for burial. I tell you the truth, wherever this gospel is preached throughout the world, what she has done will also be told, in memory of her"* (Matt. 26:10-13).

Mary's intent was pure. She wanted to honor her Lord through her offering—likely the most valuable possession she owned. The story of her bold sacrifice is told throughout the world, more than two thousand years later.

Though it was an extravagant gesture, Mary certainly wasn't aware it would be legendary in Christ's eyes. She was simply working with what she had in the context of her life. Likewise, our service to Jesus is also a type of love offering that greatly pleases Him.

And like any perfume, the odor is perceived differently. In 2 Corinthians 2:15-16, Paul tells us: *For we are to God the aroma of Christ among those who are being saved and those who are perishing. To the one we are the smell of death and to the other, the fragrance of life.*

You, too, have more to offer. Using what you already have, what fragrant offering could you pour out on Christ? On the people in your path?

Week Five - Day Two

WORTHLESS

*Let no one deceive you with empty words, for because of these things
the wrath of God comes upon the sons of disobedience* (Eph. 5:6).

The Bible makes ample use of lists--those habits and characteristics that benefit us; and those that are worthless. Paul''s letter to the Ephesians has several such lists we can use to lead and guide us in Christlike living.

Why should we pay attention to these lists in this day and age? Because they're still relevant. They're God's standard of obedience for all believers. And as Ephesians 5 says, there is a terrible fate awaiting the sons of disobedience. Our fruitfulness in serving Christ depends on our intimate relationship with Him and in obeying His commands.

Make no mistake, there are people and spiritual forces intent on stopping our progress– they want to tear us away from Jesus.

Before His crucifixion, Jesus diligently taught His disciples, preparing them for the events about to take place. He warned them, saying, *"See that no one leads you astray. For many will come in my name, saying, 'I am the Christ,' and they will lead many astray"* (Matt. 24:4-5).

Though no one knows when our Savior will come again, we can count on it in the same way we expect the sun to rise in the morning. Matthew 24 brings us a message of horror and hope. Horror for the disobedient and hope for the children of God.

Jesus' apostles and followers were full of zeal for His Word and work. Before He ascended to Heaven, He gave them a mission and purpose for living known to us as the Great Commission:

All authority in heaven and on earth has been given to me. Go therefore and make disciples of all nations, baptizing them in the name of the Father and of the Son and of the Holy Spirit, teaching them to observe all that I have commanded of you. And behold, I am with you always, to the end of the age (Matt. 28:18-20).

Jesus' promise then assures us of His presence today.

Worthless words are filled with treachery and deception. Worthless acts threaten to separate us from the one who has only the best in mind for us. If we want to be considered faithful servants and worthy of the calling He gave us and the "more" He has for us, it's imperative we pay attention to the way we live on this earth.

In your crazy busy life, what are some habits you could cultivate to better fulfill Jesus' mission of His Great Commission? In light of this pursuit, what becomes worthless in your life?

Week Five - Day Three

LIVING LIGHT

*For at one time you were darkness, but now you are light
in the Lord. Walk as children of light (for the fruit of light
is found in all that is good and right and true), and try to
discern what is pleasing to the Lord* (Eph. 5:8-10).

In ancient times, themes of light and darkness like this one we see in Ephesians 5 were common. We can find references to both of these opposites throughout the Old and New Testaments.

Of course in our plugged-in society here in the West, we don't really understand the true reality of darkness or the real power of light. With the simple flip of a switch or clap, even a word now in our smart world, a dark space instantly transforms and shadows are driven away. We quickly avoid darkness. Try asking a child (or most adults) to hang out in a pitch-black basement. The answer will be an emphatic, "No way!"

Light overcomes darkness. It comforts and brings visibility to that which is unseen.

In antiquity, the dual themes of light and darkness represent good and evil. Paul explains to his readers that a life of light in Christ produces positive results. As believers, it's up to us to discover and distinguish between what pleases God and what doesn't. Everything we need to know can be found in Christ, for He *is* the Word.

Jesus explained the "more" life we are to lead when He said, *"You are the light of the world. A city on a hill cannot be hidden. Neither do people light a lamp and put it under a bowl. Instead they put it on its stand, and it gives light to everyone in the house. In the same way, let your light shine before men, that they may see your good deeds and praise your Father in heaven"* (Matt. 5:14-16).

Opportunities to be light to the world are all around us; our communities are filled with people living in darkness. Jesus desires that we have the same compassion for those in the dark as He had for us when we were once darkness.

Maybe the elderly neighbor next door would enjoy going out for coffee. Maybe the single mother could use help with car repairs. Perhaps the veteran suffering from PTSD needs an understanding friend. Or the troubled child in your child's class could benefit from an invitation to church youth group.

Intentionally doing what we can to push back the darkness fulfills us and lightens the burdens of others. But most importantly, it pleases God and brings glory to Him.

You (yes you!) are the light of the world. Where can you be a living light today?

Week Five - Day Four

EVERYDAY MISSIONARY

For anything that becomes visible is light (Eph. 5:14).

When I was in my early twenties, I sold mineral health products for a multi-level marketing company. My belief in the company was rock-solid. After suffering an illness that left me bedridden for months, my desperate mother purchased some from a friend. Within weeks, I was not only fully healed, I also became a salesperson.

As a successful distributor, I earned my way to a regional conference. The leadership brought in an international sales speaker to help us learn about marketing psychology. At that time, much of my motivation in life was driven by the need to succeed. My illness caused me to leave college, and I felt detached from the purpose I once had.

I'm a born learner and found myself captivated by the speaker as he broke down psychology. During the middle of his discourse, he walked over to my side of the stage, looked directly at me and said, "God loves you and has a plan for your life." Then he continued on with his talk.

I was stunned! At that moment, I burst into tears, weeping silently in my seat. This random guy from Canada, just doing his job and at the same time being an everyday missionary, told me something I'd never heard before. That God loved *me* and had plans *for* me. It was as if someone turned on a light from Heaven and shined it directly into my heart.

I had to leave the room because I was a blubbering mess.

During our lunch break (still crying), I called my best friend and roommate who was the only Christian I knew personally. I felt so excited to tell her about the man and his message for me. Her response was less than stellar.

"Uh…ok," was all she said.

But her lackluster response couldn't diminish my elation. My heart completely changed that day.

The work of God is a mystery. How does He take words from a stranger and transform them into an effective force of life change? That one sentence created a hunger in me. I wanted more. I wanted to know about this mystery God and what His plans were. Instead of desiring money and success, I desired to know Him.

I'll never forget the name of this man whom God inspired to express His love. I'm eternally grateful that He didn't cave in to fear, thinking his words may be inappropriate for a business setting. He became for me a messenger of hope–a living, breathing light bearer who made God visible.

Your mission field might be right in front of your face! Who can you share God's message of love with today?

Week Five - Day Five

ORDAINED

*Therefore it says, "Awake, O sleeper, and arise from the dead,
and Christ will shine on you." Be very careful, then, how
you live—not as unwise but as wise, making the most of every
opportunity, because the days are evil. Therefore, do not be foolish,
but understand what the Lord's will is* (Eph. 5:14-17).

I adore Thomas' English muffins and for writing this particular devotion, I carb loaded for research purposes. I ate two toasted English muffins drenched in butter for your benefit. I love the company's clever and extremely appropriate well-known branding phrase: "nooks and crannies." It is the ideal description of the muffins' airy interior surface.

Once they're split open, distinct pockets appear allowing the butter (or jam) to sink in. These nooks and crannies vary in size; some are minuscule and some are large. But the purpose of each one is that the muffin gets drenched in goodness.

Likewise, our lives contain nooks and crannies—pockets of time, spaces and seasons ordained for each one of us. Paul warned his readers to be very careful and pay attention to the way they lived their lives. He urges us to wisely use the time given to us, to avoid foolish pursuits, and to live for Christ.

How do we do that? Throughout Scripture, we see that living a life of wisdom requires us to be mindful and diligent. It requires us to be intentional. At times, we can be guilty of giving more thought to our "to do" lists and holiday plans than we give to our faith. Working and resting are, of course, part of living the human life. But it's imperative we get in line with Jesus' mission and priorities.

People everywhere are living and dying without Christ. They're sleepwalking through life, unconscious of their need for Him and unaware of eternal separation. Like Jesus' disciples, we too can succumb to the temptation of drowsiness and fall into a trap of inactivity.

He urges us to wake up, to come out of our slumber and lead people into intimate relationship with Him. We can use every nook and cranny in our lives for this noble and Kingdom-advancing calling. Each day and circumstance provide us with an opportunity to shine the light of Christ for others.

Christ's sacrifice was a costly one. 1 Corinthians 6:19 reminds us: *You are not your own, for you were bought with a price. So glorify God in your body.*

God put you where you are **on** purpose and **for** a purpose–this is your mission field. He has ordained you for such a time as this.

How awake are you to the mission God has ordained for you where you live, work, learn and play?

Week Five - Day Six

SHIFT WORK

The **Fifth Shift** we need to make is to identify and begin working in our mission field.

Read through these statements and questions and think about each one thoughtfully. In your journal or notebook, record any thoughts or scripture verses that speak to you.

When Mary broke the alabaster jar over Jesus' head, the disciples were angry and Jesus was pleased. What gift could *you* offer Him?

How might your actions affect the lives of people in your life?

Would those people encourage or dissuade you?

Read over the list of habits and characteristics in Ephesians 5. Which ones exist in your life right now?

What shifts might you need to make to rid yourself of bad habits?

In your own words, what does it mean to be "children of light"?

Your mission field exists where you live, work, learn and play. What nooks and crannies (opportunities) could you engage?

Who is "right in front of your face" and needs to hear the gospel?

What method could you use to approach them?

What shift could you make to engage more fully in your mission field?

Week Six

FROM MORE STRATEGY ...
TO MORE SURRENDER

Week Six - Day One

STRENGTHENED

Finally, be strong in the Lord and in the
strength of his might (Eph. 6:10).

At the end of his letter to the Ephesians, Paul focuses our attention on the source of our strength.

We can be certain that whenever we join Jesus in His work, powerful forces will come against us. This opposition is known as spiritual warfare and it's an inevitable truth that's dangerous to diminish or ignore.

We have an Enemy, and that Enemy has designed spiritual warfare to disrupt our efforts for Christ. And while that truth is important, even more important is remembering that God who has so much more for us is victorious! Jesus' work on the cross defeated our Enemy. Yes, we still battle, but Christ has *already* won the war. We can rest in the surety of His power and might. And we can be strengthened knowing He has the last word.

One of my favorite Bible stories comes from Exodus in the Old Testament. Moses and the Israelites have fled the captivity of Pharaoh in Egypt and are camped by the Red Sea after a long journey in the wilderness.

We can only imagine the relief the escaping Hebrews must have felt as they rested. For 430 years, they had lived as slaves in Egypt. But their rest wouldn't go on for long. The Lord hardened Pharaoh's heart. Once again, the Egyptian army with their horses, chariots and weapons are after them. The Bible says that Pharaoh took "*six hundred of the best chariots, along with all the other chariots of Egypt, with officers over all of them*" (Exodus 14:7).

These notorious warriors were the best of the best and the strongest of the strong. From the camp, the Israelites saw their enemy and completely freaked out. They complained bitterly to Moses and cried out to God, immediately asking why God had led them out of exile only to be killed by Egyptian army. It was as if they all had amnesia and had lost all memory of the plagues they saw and the miracle of the passover. Moses told them to stand firm and to be fearless because God intended to save them:

The Lord will fight for you; you need only to be still" (Exodus 14:14).

Moses stretched out his hand over the Red Sea and, miracle of miracles, at once the sea parted. The Israelites walked through the sea (on dry ground) with walls of water heaped up on both sides. The Egyptians pursued them and when the last of God's people made it to the other side, Moses raised his hand again. The sea came back together, leaving no survivors.

I don't know about you, but when I'm facing opposition the last thing on my mind is stillness. The idea behind the original word "still" is inactivity. God used Pharaoh's hardened heart and attempted attack to teach both the Hebrews and the Egyptians a lesson about who is really in control. After watching the entire army drown, the Israelites trusted in the Lord and in Moses.

Times of trouble and persecution would come to God's people both then and now. Jesus gave us a heads up and then a promise of power and strength we can bank on: *"I have told you these things, so that in me you may have peace. In this world you will have trouble. But take heart! I have overcome the world"* (John 16:33).

What fear or situation do you need to hand off to the Lord today to live into your calling and be used by God?

Week Six - Day Two

ARMED

Put on the whole armor of God, that you may be able to
stand against the schemes of the devil (Eph. 6:11).

Our enemy, the devil, is a schemer. He uses cunning methods and traps to deceive people and lead them astray. Our only defense for standing (as opposed to falling) is in putting on the armor God provides and commands us to use.

The *New International Dictionary of New Testament Theology* provides a clear statement about the purpose of God's armor: "Withstanding in this armor makes it possible to stand in the evil day: The Christian life in faith is a battle in which a man may fall. To survive and to maintain one's stance, the spiritual armor is necessary. Armed with it, the believer has and occupies the position which he must maintain."

Make no mistake. The Christian life is a battle, and God alone makes us battle ready! We must use *all* of the armor He has given us and not attempt to piecemeal--a helmet of salvation here, a shield of faith there. We have full armed access to all of these divine weapons for a reason. Together, they are powerful and effective gifts we must use to be battle ready.

When military soldiers enter into conflict, they make specific preparations to withstand a variety of attacks. The battle first starts in the mind, and soldiers use various techniques to ready themselves, such as visualization, studying the enemy, and learning to control their fear.

After that, they put on their external gear. Things like helmets, Kevlar, and combat boots. Next, they pick up their weapons–rifles, machine guns, etc. They look to their commander for instructions and accept the assignments and orders given to them. No good soldier would dare enter enemy territory without being completely prepared in every area.

Likewise, no disciple should enter into conflict without the supernatural armor that God supplies to His soldiers.

We may not face physical threats (though in many places around the world Christians do), but just like he did early in Jesus' ministry, our Enemy will attack our minds, put temptations in our paths, and send messengers to torment and persecute us. These dangers are a part of our spiritual life, and they will come from both outside and *inside* the Church.

Why else would Paul talk specifically about deceitful workers and wolves in sheep's clothing who come to attack the flock? He warns the Corinthians: *"Even Satan disguises himself as an angel of light. So it is no wonder that his servants also disguise themselves as servants of righteousness* (2 Cor. 11:14-15).

How does knowing that God has provided us with all the weapons we need to arm ourselves impact how you fight our Enemy? How battle-ready are you?

Week Six - Day Three

EMPOWERED

For we do not wrestle against flesh and blood, but against
the rulers, against the authorities, against the cosmic
powers over this present darkness, against the spiritual
forces of evil in the heavenly places (Eph 6:12).

In the beginning verses of Ephesians, Paul tells us we are blessed in Christ with every spiritual blessing in the heavenly places (Eph. 1:3). So Isn't it odd to know that the cosmic powers opposing us also reside in the heavenly places?

Clarity replaces confusion when we cling to this truth: God is the Creator of everything and put all things under Christ's feet. This knowledge produces awe and reverence. It also endows us with courage to engage in the battle for souls.

The word in Greek for the collective group of rulers, authorities, cosmic powers and spiritual forces of evil is *thronos* (pronounced: throw nos). Thronos is defined as supernatural powers having some particular role in controlling the destiny and activities of human beings.

The Enemy's work is evident; we live in a time of overwhelming darkness. News stories are saturated with tales of murder, destruction and degradation. The world is engulfed in evil, and we hear witness accounts of mass killings and devastation wrought by war-mongering leaders. One of the Enemy's many tactics is using hatred and envy to tear at us and divide one another.

In verse 6:12, Paul uses the image of a wrestling match–a metaphor for an intense struggle against an opponent. Our Enemy wants to pin us to the mat and destroy us mentally, physically and spiritually.

But we don't have to worry because Jesus' Kingdom is not of this world. Neither are we. His Word is a clarion call to courage and hope. Paul tells us our enemies are not physical– they're not flesh and blood people, though Satan will sometimes use humans to accomplish his work.

When this happens, we can recall Jesus' words about the way He tells us to deal with people. He says, *"You have heard the law that says, 'Love your neighbor and hate your enemy.' But I say, love your enemies! Pray for those who persecute you! In that way, you will be acting as true children of your Father in heaven. For he gives his sunlight to both the evil and the good, and he sends rain on the just and the unjust alike"* (Matt 5:43-45).

Our weapons equip and empower us to overcome our adversary: *For the weapons of our warfare are not of the flesh but have divine power to destroy strongholds* (2 Cor. 10:4).

How effectively are you using the weapons of our warfare against our Enemy? What changes can you make in your daily rhythms to feel and act more equipped and empowered?

Week Six - Day Four

DRESSED AND READY

*Therefore, take up the whole armor of God, that you may be able to
withstand in the evil day, and having done all, to stand firm. Stand
therefore, having fastened on the belt of truth, and having put on
the breastplate of righteousness, and, as shoes for your feet, having
put on the readiness given by the gospel of peace. In all circumstances
take up the shield of faith, with which you can extinguish all the
flaming darts of the evil one; and take the helmet of salvation, and
the sword of the Spirit, which is the word of God, praying at all times
in the Spirit, with all prayer and supplication* (Eph. 6:13-17).

I love this vivid image of a warrior dressing for combat. Every piece of armor is accounted for; nothing is left on the battlefield. As warriors, we're clothed with heavenly protection and championed by Jesus Himself.

Our divine commander sends us into active battle wanting us to experience the victory of His Son. As a reminder, let's revisit this powerful scripture: *And He put all things under his feet and gave him as head over all things to the church, which is His body, the fullness of Him, who fills all in all (*Eph. 1:22-23).

Engaging in battle and armed in our protective gear provides us with *full* coverage. The outer wear (belt, breastplate, shoes, shield and helmet) are our defensive weapons that protect our inner self from assault. What's under attack is our belief in the truth, our standing in righteousness, our faith and the assurance of our salvation.

We must win at all costs!

There are amazing books, Bible studies and blogs we can read that focus on the individual pieces of armor, so I won't delve deeply into all the armor of God. But here in this last chapter, I want to focus on our one offensive weapon–the sword of the Spirit.

Everything we need to live a victorious life is contained in God's Word. The Bible is God's story, our guidebook for life, and a weapon of truth. Of course, no one's going to appreciate us wielding it like a hammer and beating them over the head with it. But we do use it to learn about God, teach about Him and share His message with the world.

Hebrews 4:12 tells us: *For the word of God is living and active, sharper than any two-edged sword, piercing to the division of soul and of spirit, of joints and of marrow, and discerning the thoughts and intentions of the heart.*

The Christian faith is active and effective for God's purpose. Just look at the action words Paul uses when instructing us: Take up. Stand firm. Put on.

Being dressed and ready prepares us for a life of vitality and fullness in Christ. It prepares us to live the abundant, "made for more" life God has for His people. We don't put on all this armor to sit on the couch or hide in obscurity. We do it so we can fight on the mission field our commander has assigned and called us to...

We are warriors. How dressed and ready for war are you?

Week Six - Day Five

ON ALERT

*To that end, keep alert with all perseverance, making supplication
for all the saints and also for me, that words may be given to
me in opening my mouth boldly to proclaim the mystery of the
gospel, for which I am an ambassador in chains, that I may
declare it boldly, as I ought to speak (Eph. 6:18-20).*

It can be easy to compare ourselves to others and end up feeling insignificant. We live in a world that judges our worth based on the things we achieve, numbers of social media followers and how much money we earn. Please remember that these meaningless metrics have no merit in God's kingdom. They never have, and they never will.

Look at Paul. He was an ordinary man whose encounter with Jesus transformed him into an extraordinary one. His relationship with Jesus and completing the task assigned to him was all that mattered—to him and to God.

He wrote these words to the Philippians: *Yes, everything else is worthless when compared with the infinite value of knowing Christ Jesus my Lord. For his sake, I have discarded everything else, counting it all as garbage, so that I could gain Christ* (Eph. 3:8).

Paul's love for Christ and the Church served as the driving force for all his activity. We see him as a champion of faith (and he was), but he never forgot the source of his strength, his need for the Lord, and to ask for the prayers of fellow believers.

When facing possible danger or emergency, alertness is critical. For example, my son recently got his learner's driving permit and pesters me to let him drive me around town. Admittedly, I can tell you I don't enjoy this—at all. I feel helpless and nervous in the passenger seat. Each time we go for a drive, I cover us in prayers of safety. During these rides, my senses are heightened, and I'm hyper aware of all the possibilities for danger.

As believers, we should arm ourselves with alertness at all times. In fact, Scripture tells us to do just that: *Stay alert! Watch out for your great enemy, the devil. He prowls around like a roaring lion, looking for someone to devour* (1 Peter 5:8).

Like Paul, God has assigned each one of us the task of making disciples. We're to go out into the world boldly proclaiming the Good News of Jesus and His kingdom.

So let's push fear aside and take comfort in Jesus' words in John as we go out to serve Him:

I am leaving you with a gift—peace of mind and heart. And the peace I give is a gift the world cannot give. So don't be troubled or afraid (John 14:27).

What steps can you take to increase your level of alertness?

Week Six - Day Six

SHIFT WORK

The **Sixth (and final) Shift** we need to make is to recognize that we have a powerful enemy and get prepared for battle.

Read through these statements and questions and think about each one thoughtfully. In your journal or notebook, record any thoughts or scripture verses that speak to you.

Reflect on a time when you were in a precarious position and God came to your rescue. Write about it in your journal.

What's your natural response when facing difficulty and why?

In what way do you see the Enemy's schemes play out in your life?

How battle-ready are you? What shifts do you need to make to prepare?

In what way is your local church preparing you for spiritual warfare?

Scripture tells us we do not wrestle against "flesh and blood." List the four supernatural forces working against us.

Write about the particular way our spiritual Enemy uses human enemies in your life.

Jesus commands us to love our enemies and pray for them. If you have one (or more) enemy, write out a specific prayer for them.

List any pieces of spiritual armor you may be missing.

Other believers are our brothers and sisters in arms. Share the names of believers you will commit to praying over.

About the Author

ERIKA RIZKALLAH is a wife, mother and entrepreneur. In 2009, she left her job in vocational ministry and ran away from home (with her family) to live on an island in North Carolina. Now she spends her time writing, running a small business and sweeping sand out of everything.

Endnotes

Introduction: Wilson, Todd, and Rob Wegner. *Made For More: Six Essential Shifts for Creating a Culture of Mobilization*. Exponential, 2018.

Week One - Day One: King, Bob. "9,096 Stars in the Sky – Is That All?" *Sky and Telescope Magazine*, 17 Sept. 2014.

Week One - Day Four: Youngblood, Ronald F, et al., editors. *Nelson's New Illustrated Bible Dictionary*. Thomas Nelson Publishers, 1995.

Week Two - Day One: Morgan, Thad. "Are You Prepared for a Zombie Apocalypse? The U.S. Government Is." *History.com*, 31 Oct. 2017, http:/history.com.

Week Two - Day Three: Louw, Johannes P, and Eugene A Nida. *Greek-English Lexicon of the New Testament Based on Semantic Domains*. United Bible Societies, 1988.

Week Two - Day Five: *Supreme Court of the United States*, http:/supremecourt.gov.

Week Three - Day Three: Wilson, Todd. *More*. Zondervan, 2016.

Week Six - Day Two: Verbrugge, Verlyn D, editor. *New International Dictionary of New Testament Theology: Abridged Edition*. Zondervan, 2000.

Week Six - Day Three: Louw, Johannes P, and Eugene A Nida. *Greek-English Lexicon of the New Testament Based On Semantic Domains*. United Bible Societies, 1988.

Made in the
USA
Monee, IL